**RUSH**
*Lights, Camera, Action!*
**HOUR** 1 2 3

# RUSH HOUR

## Lights, Camera, Action!

# 1 2 3

**Introduction by Brett Ratner**

A NEWMARKET PICTORIAL MOVIEBOOK

This book is published in the United States of America.

FIRST EDITION

10 9 8 7 6 5 4 3 2 1
ISBN: 978-1-55704-783-0 (Paperback)

10 9 8 7 6 5 4 3 2 1
ISBN: 978-1-55704-784-7 (Hardcover)

Grateful acknowledgment is made for permission to reproduce the following images:
Page 9: Phil Stern photos © Courtesy of Phil Stern/CPi. Reprinted by permission.
Page 15: *New York Observer* cartoon © by R.J. Matson, *The New York Observer,* 2001. Reprinted by permission.
Page 18: *TIME* Magazine cover "Mr. Hollywood—Jackie Chan" 10/19/88 © 1988 Time, Inc. Reprinted by permission.

Library of Congress Cataloging-in-Publication Data available upon request.

QUANTITY PURCHASES
Companies, professional groups, clubs, and other organizations may qualify for special terms when ordering quantities of this title. For information or to obtain our catalog, write Special Sales Department, Newmarket Press, 18 East 48th Street, New York, NY 10017; call (212) 832-3575; fax (212) 832-3629; or e-mail info@newmarketpress.com.

www.newmarketpress.com

Manufactured in the United States of America.

Other Newmarket Pictorial Moviebooks include:

*Dreamgirls: The Movie Musical*
*The Namesake: A Portrait of the Film Based on the Novel by Jhumpa Lahiri*
*The Art of X-Men The Last Stand: From Concept to Feature Film*
*Tim Burton's Corpse Bride: An Invitation to the Wedding*
*Memoirs of a Geisha: A Portrait of the Film*
*Kingdom of Heaven: The Ridley Scott Film and the History Behind the Story*
*Ray: A Tribute to the Movie, the Music, and the Man*
*Vanity Fair: Bringing Thackeray's Timeless Novel to the Screen*
*Two Brothers: A Fable on Film and How It Was Told*
*Van Helsing: The Making of the Legend*
*Cold Mountain: The Journey from Book to Film*
*In America: A Portrait of the Film*
*The Hulk: The Illustrated Screenplay*
*The Art of X2: The Collector's Edition*
*The Art of X2: The Making of the Blockbuster Film*
*Chicago: From Stage to Screen—The Movie and Illustrated Lyrics*
*Catch Me If You Can: The Film and the Filmmakers*
*Frida: Bringing Frida Kahlo's Life and Art to Film*
*E.T. The Extra-Terrestrial: From Concept to Classic*
*Planet of the Apes: Re-imagined by Tim Burton*
*Moulin Rouge: The Splendid Book That Charts the Journey of Baz Luhrmann's Motion Picture*
*The Art of The Matrix*
*Gladiator: The Making of the Ridley Scott Epic*
*Crouching Tiger, Hidden Dragon: A Portrait of the Ang Lee Film*

INTRODUCTION

**by Brett Ratner**

Since I was eight years old, my dream was to become a movie director. I would've been content making Super 8 films in the backyard with my friends for the rest of my life. Never did I imagine that I would direct a movie that would turn into a franchise lasting ten years, entertaining people across the globe and starring one of the funniest comedic duos in the history of cinema.

I was twenty-six years old when I directed the film *Money Talks*, an action comedy starring Chris Tucker and Charlie Sheen. The film cost $20 million to make and ended up grossing double that.

I noticed that kids were purchasing tickets for PG-rated movies, yet sneaking into my R-rated *Money Talks*. So I decided to make a PG-13 action comedy with Chris Tucker. Because of my exposure to hip hop and my love for kung fu movies, I came up with the idea of pairing Chris Tucker with Jackie Chan. I knew that the combination of Jackie's physical humor and Chris's verbal humor would be phenomenal.

There have to be certain ingredients in a script to make a worthwhile action buddy comedy. The first is to create a fish-out-of-water situation for the characters. *Beverly Hills Cop* is a perfect example of the fish-out-of-water concept with the tone of a thriller, thus creating the perfect action comedy.

*ABOVE: Brett Ratner directing his stellar cast Chris Tucker and Jackie Chan. RIGHT: Original "clappers" from all three* Rush Hour *films.*

Another crucial factor is the "worthy villain." Take Albert Ganz (played by James Remar) in *48 Hours*, a character audiences believed was a real threat. These types of choices differentiate an action comedy from a broad comedy. Finally, there has to be great chemistry between the main characters, such as De Niro and Grodin in *Midnight Run*. In my search for the ideal script, I came across many that would fit into a buddy action comedy, but they were all too broad. I wanted the tone of the film to be more of a thriller, and the comedy to come from the situations and characters, not from the jokes.

When I discovered the script for *Rush Hour*, I felt it was the perfect vehicle for what I had in mind. It read more like an action movie than a comedy, and I knew I could adapt it for Chris and Jackie. I wanted to work with Chris again, so I asked him if he was a fan of Jackie Chan's. Naturally he was, and that sent me on my mission: Find Jackie Chan and convince him to do *Rush Hour*. It turned out that Jackie was in South Africa filming a movie called *Who Am I?* Amazingly, he agreed to meet me. In no time I would be on a plane from L.A. to South Africa to meet Jackie for lunch.

I did my homework and watched every Jackie Chan movie for the tenth time. I read every article I could find on him. During the twenty-six hour journey to South Africa, I was so excited I was going to meet this Hong Kong

*BELOW: Soundtrack covers from* Rush Hour *and* Rush Hour 2. *Brett Ratner with composer Lalo Schifrin.*

*ABOVE: Producer Roger Birnbaum (in yellow), Producer Arthur Sarkissian (white turtleneck), with Brett Ratner and Werner Herzog on the* Rush Hour *set.*

legend that I couldn't sleep. As I read article after article, I started to feel queasy and began to realize that my dream of getting Jackie Chan to do *Rush Hour* might be just that, a dream. In one of the articles I read, Jackie vowed that he would never make another American film because of his bad experiences working with American action directors. His dream had been to be an American movie star, but his role in *The Cannonball Run* (1981) turned out to be the worst experience of his life. At that time Jackie Chan was a huge star in Asia and relatively unknown in the States. On set, Jackie was disregarded by Burt Reynolds, Sammy Davis Jr., and Dean Martin. They didn't know who he was or his true value. He was not included in the American marketing campaign, but was prominently featured on the Asian movie poster. After seeing the film, his Asian fans were terribly dis-

appointed that Burt Reynolds, not Jackie Chan, turned out to be the star of the movie.

When I finally landed in Johannesburg, I was astounded to see Jackie Chan himself waiting at the gate for me! He looked even more surprised than I was; when I walked up to him, he thought I was a fan and certainly not the director coming to meet him personally. He surprised me again when he drove us to the restaurant in a van himself. He didn't say a word. I, of course, after no sleep, immediately launched into my pitch, telling him how I had just watched all of his movies again and couldn't wait to cast him in *Rush Hour*. I explained that I knew why his experiences with *The Cannonball Run*, *The Big Brawl*, and *The Protector* hadn't worked in the United States and had alienated his core Asian audience. I told him I knew how to make a film that would deliver to the American audience and keep his Asian fans satisfied.

I admitted that I could never deliver action that would compare to *Police Story* or his *Project A* series. If I wanted to make a true hybrid of Hong Kong filmmaking, I would focus on the characters but leave the action up to him. It was very bold of me to say that I personally loved

*BELOW: Behind-the-scenes images taken on the* Rush Hour *set by esteemed photographer Phil Stern.*

*ABOVE: (from left to right) Producer Jay Stern, Brett Ratner, Chris Tucker, First Assistant Director Jamie Freitag, and Jackie Chan.*

watching a twenty-minute Jackie Chan fight sequence, but that it would not fly with American audiences. We would have to take that same twenty-minute fight and cut it down to the best two minutes. As I saw it, American audiences were going to the movies to fall in love with the characters and the story, while Hong Kong audiences were primarily satisfied with great action. I also told him that in most of his movies, his stunt men played the roles of villains. American audiences want to connect with the villain as much as the hero. I wanted to surround him with real actors in an atmosphere of a thriller, but keep his physical comedy throughout.

I realized I had talked too much, while Jackie had just nodded and politely smiled. I had been far too confident and felt I had blown it before I had gotten a real chance to sell him my idea. I knew for sure Jackie was not going to tell me right away if he would be willing to do the movie, and because of his noncommittal demeanor, it was impossible to tell what he was thinking of me or my idea.

I also knew that according to Chinese custom, whatever Jackie offered me at the restaurant could not be turned down or he would be offended. The first thing he put in front of me was wine—extremely expensive wine, a bottle of 1982 Chateau Petrus. I had never had a glass of alcohol in my life, but I pretended to drink by swishing the wine in the back of my mouth and then spitting it back into the glass. I was also

presented with a huge slab of abalone—shellfish. It didn't look edible but I was desperate to connect with Jackie, so I swallowed piece after piece without chewing, just smiling away. I hoped that my enjoyment of the abalone would ingratiate me to Jackie, because my pitch definitely wasn't working. Jackie had not seen *Money Talks* and didn't know Chris Tucker, but I assured him that Chris's fast talking combined with Jackie's physical comedy would be a great match.

Jackie was impressed with my knowledge of Hong Kong cinema, but I started to feel my pitch wasn't convincing him. He had made movies for longer than I had been alive. I think he was most struck by my sincerity when I handed him the script of *Rush Hour* and told him that I loved the idea of the movie, but I thought it was a terrible script. I put myself on the line and told him what I really thought: "Basically, the script sucks, but I know what I want to do with it." I was going to hire a talented young writer named Jeff Nathanson to rewrite the script.

I left lunch without a clue about Jackie's response. At least I was going to be able to tell my future grandchildren about the time I flew to South Africa just to have lunch with Jackie Chan. A week later, my agent called and gave me the news: Jackie Chan was going to do *Rush Hour*. The dream became a reality when

*LEFT: President of New Line Productions Toby Emmerich and Brett Ratner.*

**What audiences most responded to is the chemistry between Chris and Jackie. The two of them together is like an explosion in a bottle.**

I finally introduced Jackie to Chris.

Chris expressed his enthusiasm for Jackie and admiration for his work. And Jackie graciously articulated his excitement about us working together. After the meeting, Chris asked me to walk him outside. As soon as we stepped out of the door, he said, "I really like Jackie Chan, but he doesn't speak a word of English." I reassured him that everything would be fine. When I went back in and asked Jackie what he thought about Chris, he said, "I really like him, but I don't understand anything he's saying." I knew right then and there that they were going to be great together. With their language barrier and fondness for each other, I knew that when I turned the cameras on, the element that is so vital to making a successful buddy action picture would flood the screen: CHEMISTRY. To this day, I believe that Jackie and Chris still don't understand the words coming out of each other's mouths, but what they do understand is what makes a great on-screen duo.

*Rush Hour* is an amalgamation of Hong Kong action, buddy cop films, fish-out-of-water comedy, a great villain, and a brilliant Lalo Schifrin score. To me, Lalo is as important as the main actors. I wanted to work with him long be-

fore I ever became a director. My favorite score is from the Bruce Lee classic *Enter the Dragon*, which was a big inspiration because it mixed funky urban grooves with Chinese instrumentations. Lalo created a score for *Rush Hour* that has elements of his 70s coolness with an updated, hard-edged action tone. It's evocative and propelling, threatening and thrilling all at once. Lalo's music is a character unto its own.

I must give a tremendous amount of credit to my collaborators, all filmmakers in their own right. My assistant director/co-producer, Jamie Freitag, has stood by my side through all three *Rush Hour* films and is an integral part of the creation and execution. My editor, Mark Helfrich, has edited all eight of my feature films. He has sifted through millions of feet of film and has helped me to craft films with a

*ABOVE: Promotional items from* Rush Hour 2. *BELOW: (left to right) First Assistant Director Jamie Freitag, Brett Ratner, and Tom Wilkinson on the set of* Rush Hour.

consistent style and a great pace and tone that make the *Rush Hour* films the success they are. Mark never stops surprising me with his talent and has just directed his first feature film. My producers, Arthur Sarkissian, Roger Birnbaum, Jon Glickman, and Jay Stern have supported my vision on every level. Jay was an executive at New Line responsible for hiring me to direct my first film, *Money Talks*, and eventually became my partner and producer at Rat Entertainment. My line producer, Andy Davis, has been a true collaborator and creative partner on *Rush Hour 2* and *3*, never saying no to my ideas while still finding a way to keep the studio happy. Jeff Nathanson, my writer, breathed life into the script and created dynamic characters for Jackie and Chris to embrace. There is no one better suited to capture the voices of Carter and Lee. Jeff is a talented director in his own right and also one of the funniest writers on earth. Aside from the three *Rush Hour* films, Jeff wrote *Catch Me If You Can*, *The Terminal*, and *Indiana Jones 4*.

My three cinematographers, Adam Greenberg, Matt Leonetti, and Jimmy Muro, gave each *Rush Hour* a distinctive look and yet remained true to the story. As I was shooting *Rush Hour 2*, I stumbled onto the set of *Lethal Weapon 4* and watched the second unit director, Conrad Palmisano, work. As I observed him, I noticed the action he filmed was not about the stunts but about the story. Conrad became my stunt co-

*ABOVE: Producer Andy Davis and Brett Ratner on the set of* Rush Hour 3.

ordinator and second unit director on *Rush Hour 2* and *3*. He successfully merged Hong Kong action with Western comedy, never compromising either genre. He is a true filmmaker, who has the understanding of what it takes to create a great action sequence and never deviate from the story or the tone of the film.

Hundreds of crew members have contributed to the success of *Rush Hour*—all with incomparable passion, hard work, and enthusiasm. I'd like to thank Mike Weldon, the best camera assistant in the world. The omnipresent Brad Einhorn, the greatest propman in the movie business. Production designers Robb Wilson King, Terence Marsh, and Edward Verreaux for their beautiful sets. Also my great team of assis-

*ABOVE: A* Rush Hour *cartoon in the* New York Observer, *signed by Bill Clinton. BELOW: (left to right) Associate Producer David Gorder, Producer Arthur Sarkissian, and Screenwriter Jeff Nathanson.*

tant editors, Chris Jackson, Laura Steiger, Peggy Eghbalian, and my talented editors of *Rush Hour 3*, Don and Dean Zimmerman. My genius costume designers, Betsy Heimann, Rita Ryack, and Sharen Davis. John Bruno, the visual effects supervisor on *Rush Hour 3*, who made me realize that nothing is impossible. *Rush Hour*'s fearless stunt coordinators, Terry Leonard and Eddie Braun, who collaborated incredibly with the Jackie Chan stunt team. And the Jackie Chan stunt team, a group whose endless work ethic and dedication to the art of action are inspiring. Of course, David Gorder, for his tireless effort in putting this book together. Also I want to thank Anita Chang, my loyal assistant of many years to whom I'm forever grateful.

In addition, I'd like to thank the stellar actors who contributed their talent to the *Rush Hour* series: Tom Wilkinson, Elizabeth Peña, Chris Penn, Ken Leung, Tzi Ma, Harris Yulin, Ziyi Zhang, John Lone, Roselyn Sanchez, Alan King, Max von Sydow, Hiroyuki Sanada, Yvan Attal, Youki Kudoh, Noémie Lenoir, and my favorite director, Roman Polanski.

*OPPOSITE: Jackie Chan and Chris Tucker take Paris by storm in* Rush Hour 3. *ABOVE: Editor Mark Helfrich and Brett Ratner with Jackie Chan. BELOW: Notable* Rush Hour *props from the Brett Ratner collection.*

I would especially like to thank Bob Shaye for giving me creative support and a blank check, and Michael Lynne for always saying yes when Bob said no. Also, Toby Emmerich for his ideas and writing on *Rush Hour 2* and his perseverance in making *Rush Hour 3* a reality. Russell Schwartz and Laura Carillo for their brilliant marketing. Rolf Mittweig for making the franchise an international success and sending us around the world. David Tuckerman for always getting us the most screens on the right date. Ben Zinkin, Judd Funk, and Stefanie Markman for always getting the deals done. Leon Dudevoir for never shutting me down, Brent Kaviar for always protecting the quality of the films, and Jody Levin for helping us make it through our insane post schedules. Paul Broucek for always getting fat budgets for music. Christina Kounelias, Elissa Greer, John Smith, and Claire Anne Conlon for always getting us the best publicity and promotion, and everyone at New Line for working so hard and caring so much. Sammy and Victor Hadida for their inspired idea to bring *Rush Hour* to France. I can't thank Mike DeLuca enough. He believed in my talent from the beginning, hired me to direct my first feature film, and green-lit my second . . . *RUSH HOUR.*

# 1 + 1 + 1 = 7!
## A MOST LUCKY COMBINATION!

**JACKIE CHAN** is an international superstar whose achievements and talents remain unparalleled after a thirty-year career in the movie business. His name is synonymous with breathtaking stunts and side-splitting physical humor, and his popularity has continued to grow as he expands his reach beyond Asia and the Americas to touch audiences worldwide.

Born in Hong Kong in 1954, Jackie was enrolled in the Peking Opera School at the age of seven, where he was trained in acrobatics, gymnastics, dance, singing, and drama. Upon graduation from the Academy, Jackie found work hard to come by as the popularity of Chinese Opera dwindled. Like many of his schoolmates, Jackie joined the movie world as an extra and an occasional stuntman. As his talent became obvious to producers and directors, he quickly moved up the ranks and was soon coordinating stunts in Hong Kong films. After the untimely death of Bruce Lee, Jackie was groomed as a replacement for Lee, but rejected that idea when he realized that his own brand of humor and stunt work would be his ace in the hole. In 1978 he single-handedly changed the Hong Kong film industry by combining humor with clever stunt work in movies such as *Snake in the Eagle's Shadow* and *Drunken Master*.

In 1980, Jackie directed his first film, *Young Master*, and its runaway success secured his future as a legend in the Hong Kong film industry. Jackie then tried his hand at several American productions, but results were disappointing and he returned to Hong Kong. However, he took some of what he'd learned in America and applied it to Hong Kong film projects with brilliant results. Enamored of great comedic legends such as Buster Keaton and Charlie Chaplin, Jackie created his own unique brand of physical comedy, which was extremely successful in Asia and which became increasingly noticed by American mov-

iegoers. After the success of 1995's *Rumble in the Bronx*, followed by the *Rush Hour* series, *Shanghai Noon*, and *Shanghai Knights*, Jackie became a true international superstar.

Although he is well known for his work in front of the camera, Jackie also has a long list of credits behind the scenes, working for many years as producer, director, and stunt coordinator. In 2004, he began his own production company, Jackie Chan Emperor Movies, Ltd. He has been the recipient of countless awards for his work, including a Best Actor award for his dramatic role in 2004's *New Police Story*.

Known worldwide for his cinematic work, Jackie has a side to him which is not as well known—that of a philanthropist. In 1988, he founded the Jackie Chan Charitable Foundation in Hong Kong and since then has worked tirelessly for many and varied charitable causes. Most recently he has created the Dragon's Heart Foundation, which uses donations to build schools in poor and remote regions of China. When he is not filming, Jackie travels to these areas to deliver supplies, supervise the planning of schools, and lend support to the children and their parents.

Jackie's lifetime of devotion to the film industry has garnered him countless awards. He has been voted The World's Most Popular Movie Star by *Time* magazine, been honored with a star on Hollywood's Walk of Fame, had his handprints installed at Grauman's Chinese Theatre, received several honorary professorships, and been the recipient of countless ambassadorships and film awards. Jackie's future plans include getting back to directing, trying his hand at more varied movie roles, and continuing his charity work. With the unending support of his fans from nearly every country in the world, Jackie's illustrious career shows no signs of slowing down.

## + CHRIS TUCKER

is hailed as one of the funniest comics around, and has come a long way since his stand-up comedy days on *Def Comedy Jam*. Starring in box-office smashes that include the number-one grossing comedy in 2001, *Rush Hour 2*, as well as *Friday*, *Dead Presidents*, *Money Talks*, and the original *Rush Hour* (which has grossed $250 million worldwide), Tucker has clearly proved himself to be one of Hollywood's hottest talents. With his unique voice, fast-paced humor, and animated facial expressions, Tucker entertains all audiences and has left a lasting impression on the American psyche.

In honor of his proven track record of power as a box-office funnyman, the world's theater owners named Tucker Comedy Star of the Year at 2001 ShoWest.

In 2002, Tucker traveled to Africa, along with U2 singer Bono and U.S. Secretary of the Treasury Paul O'Neill, on a fact-finding mission to see how U.S. money would help the African countries wrecked by AIDS, unsanitary living conditions, and hunger. Deeply affected by what he saw, Tucker has since been a diplomat of sorts, making it his mission to continue to raise awareness and money to combat the AIDS crisis in Africa. In recognition of his record of accomplishments and his potential to contribute to shap-

*Lights, Camera, Action!*

*Lights, Camera, Action!*

ing the future of the world, Tucker was recently made a Young Global Leader by the Forum of Young Global Leaders.

"The great thing about Chris Tucker," says Jonathan Glickman, producer of the *Rush Hour* series, "is that he's totally unafraid to play somebody who doesn't always get the girl or doesn't always save the day. He likes to make fun of himself. And so while he is a great dramatic actor, he has a great sense of fun. He also has an intensity that magnifies the screen. When he wants to be funny, all eyes are on him. When he wants to be serious, all eyes are on him. That's what makes him a movie star. He's just a regular guy who happens to be hilarious, and happens to be good-looking, and happens to have a lot of fun."

*ABOVE: (left to right) Chris Tucker, Michael Weldon, Brett Ratner, and Jackie Chan on the set of* Rush Hour 2.

## + BRETT RATNER

has established himself as one of Hollywood's most successful directors in a very short time. Ratner's seven feature films have grossed over $1 billion worldwide. At twenty-six years old he directed his first feature film, the surprise box-office hit *Money Talks*, a comedy starring Charlie Sheen and Chris Tucker. His second film, the action comedy *Rush Hour*, starred Jackie Chan and Chris Tucker and earned $250 million worldwide. He followed that success with the romantic fantasy drama *The Family Man*, a critical and box-office hit starring Nicolas Cage and Téa Leoni. A year later, Ratner delivered Hong Kong–style action with Chan and Tucker in the hit sequel, *Rush Hour 2*, which grossed more than $342 million worldwide. Ratner made his first foray into the world of suspense thrillers with his fifth feature film, *Red Dragon*, the *Silence of the Lambs* prequel starring Edward Norton, Anthony Hopkins, Ralph Fiennes, Philip Seymour Hoffman, and Emily Watson. Ratner's sixth feature film, *After the Sunset*, starring Pierce Brosnan, Salma Hayek, Woody Harrelson, and Don Cheadle, enjoyed success in theatres nationwide.

Ratner recently shattered several box-office records with his latest release, *X-Men: The Last Stand*,

the third installment in the popular film series based on the *X-Men* comic books. The film opened with a staggering $123 million in just four days. It was the biggest Memorial Day weekend in history, even exceeding the previous Memorial Day weekend benchmark, *The Lost World: Jurassic Park*'s $90.2 million in 1997. Its $45.1 million opening day marked the second-biggest single-day box office ever, and the film has grossed more than $450 million worldwide thus far. Starring Patrick Stewart, Hugh Jackman, Ian McKellen,

*Lights, Camera, Action!*

ABOVE: *Brett Ratner and Roman Polanski on the set of* Rush Hour 3.

and Halle Berry, the feature focuses on the ongoing war between the X-Men and the Brotherhood, a band of powerful mutants organized under Xavier's former ally, Magneto.

Raised in Miami Beach, Ratner had dreamed of being a filmmaker since the age of eight. He enrolled in New York University's Tisch School of the Arts at age sixteen, becoming the department's youngest film major. While attending NYU Film School, he made *Whatever Happened to Mason Reese*, a short film starring and about the former child actor. The award-winning project received funding from Steven Spielberg's Amblin Entertainment. Ratner's big break came after he screened his film for hip-hop impresario Russell Simmons, launching a successful career in music videos. He has directed more than 100 videos since then for artists including Madonna, Mariah Carey, Jessica Simpson, Jay-Z, Wu Tang Clan, D'Angelo, Heavy D, Mary J. Blige, Foxy Brown, Public Enemy, P. Diddy, and many others.

Ratner won the MTV Video Music Award for Best Video for a Film for Madonna's "Beautiful Stranger" from the *Austin Powers* soundtrack. In addition, Ratner received an MTV Movie Award for Best Fight Sequence for *Rush Hour 2* as well as a Tony Award for producing Russell Simmons' *Def Poetry Jam* on Broadway. Ratner was the recipient of the Spirit of Chrysalis Award for his dedication and leadership in helping economically disadvantaged and homeless individuals change their lives through jobs. He is currently on the boards of Chrysalis and Best Buddies and serves on the Dean's Council of the NYU Tisch School of the Arts.

In addition to success in film and music, Ratner has also segued into the world of book publishing. He published the controversial book *Naked Pictures of My Ex-Girlfriends*, by Mark Helfrich, and authored *Hilhaven Lodge: The Photo Booth Pictures*, which was released in October 2003.

Brett has recently ventured into still photography, and his photographs have appeared in *Vanity Fair* and have graced the covers of *Vogue Homme* and *V-Life*. In addition, he has shot the fashion campaigns for Baby Phat, Jimmy Choo, and Jordache Jeans. Brett Ratner currently resides in Los Angeles.

## = THE PERFECT SCREEN TEAM

Director Brett Ratner says: "Jackie and Chris have the kind of chemistry I can't create—either it exists or it doesn't. The magic really comes from the fact that they have such love and affection for each other. That's what makes their dynamic so interesting. It's undeniable. It's up on the screen. There's nothing the director could do, the writer could do. It just exists.

"The two of them together are like an explosion in a bottle. Chris Tucker is a master of verbal comedy. Jackie Chan is a master of physical comedy. Their talents work together and make sense. Chris makes Jackie laugh; Jackie makes Chris laugh. Ultimately, it's the perfect marriage. These two guys love each other.

"So I'm not just the director—I'm a fan, too. I'm a fan of Chris Tucker; I'm a fan of Jackie Chan. I have such admiration for them. They make me laugh. They make me smile. And I love to capture that. We're having fun making the movie. You can see it up there on the screen."

Chris Tucker says: "Jackie Chan and I were born to work together. We're best buddies and we fight just alike. We're like brothers, only I'm black and he's Chinese."

*When Chris and Jackie started acting together on the set of the first* Rush Hour, *you knew something pretty special was going on. Between Brett and Chris and Jackie it was like one plus one plus one equals seven.*

—PRODUCER JAY STERN

23

RUSH HOUR 1

HONG KONG / L.A.

# DETECTIVE INSPECTOR LEE is the pride of the Royal Hong Kong Police—a

tough, dedicated cop whose modest demeanor gives no hint that he is also a martial arts genius. His favorite pupil is the Chinese Consul's eleven-year-old daughter, for whom he is both bodyguard and best friend. His assignment: go to America and rescue her when she is kidnapped by the criminal mastermind who killed Lee's partner. Unwilling to have their kidnapping investigation hampered by a meddling outsider, the FBI assigns rogue LAPD detective James Carter to the case. Carter is a nightmare to his superiors—reckless, arrogant, and too infuriating to even have a partner.

Seizing the case as an opportunity to impress the FBI and ultimately join the Bureau, Carter enthusiastically accepts his assignment—until he discovers that his mission is to "baby-sit" Lee and keep him away from the investigation at any cost. In a move that is vintage Carter, the detective covertly embarks on a one-man crusade to solve the case. Of course, he must first distract Inspector Lee.

Within hours, Carter realizes he has greatly underestimated his Hong Kong counterpart, who has quickly seen through his ruse, given Carter the slip, and landed in the middle of the FBI's investigation.

As the impatient FBI agents try to cast off these unwanted misfits, cultures clash, tempers flare, and entire city blocks are leveled before these two cops from two very different worlds join forces to save the young girl.

Together with the help of LAPD bomb expert Tania Johnson, Carter and Lee wreak havoc on Los Angeles and the FBI investigation as they become tangled in a deadly web of revenge, deceit, and betrayal.

*ABOVE: Restaurateur Michael Chow
(Mr. Chow) in his first* Rush Hour *movie, with
Diana Weng, Jackie Chan's dialogue coach.*

CARTER: Ooh, that's tight, that's beautiful, that's nice — what's that?

CLIVE: C-4.

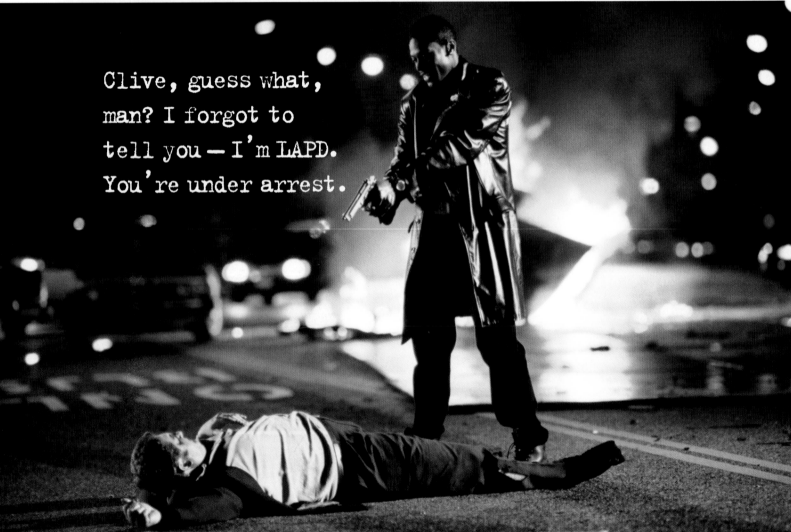

Clive, guess what, man? I forgot to tell you — I'm LAPD. You're under arrest.

'm like Muhammad Ali and Brett's like my trainer, Bundini Brown. He keeps pushing and pushing. He knows he can get it out of you, and in a couple of takes you get so upset that then it comes out. And he says, "Okay, move on." He listens to me and I listen to him. We work as a team because we're good friends and we can say anything to each other.

**—CHRIS TUCKER**

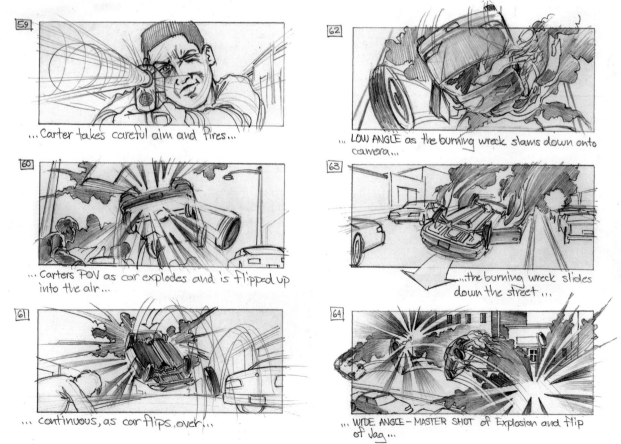

59 ...Carter takes careful aim and fires...

60 ...Carters POV as car explodes and is flipped up into the air...

61 ...continuous, as car flips over...

62 ...LOW ANGLE as the burning wreck slams down onto camera...

63 ...the burning wreck slides down the street...

64 ...WIDE ANGLE – MASTER SHOT of Explosion and flip of Jag...

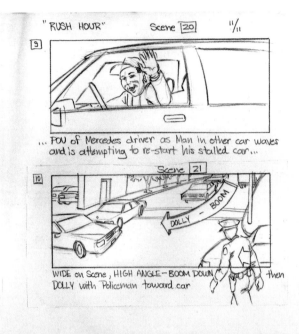

"RUSH HOUR"   Scene 20   11/11

...POV of Mercedes driver as Man in other car waves and is attempting to re-start his stalled car...

Scene 21

WIDE on Scene, HIGH ANGLE—BOOM DOWN then DOLLY with Policeman toward car

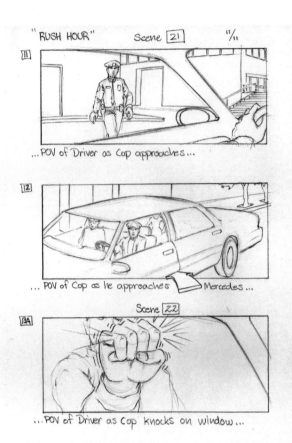

"RUSH HOUR"   Scene 21   11/11

...POV of Driver as Cop approaches...

...POV of Cop as he approaches Mercedes...

Scene 22

...POV of Driver as Cop knocks on window...

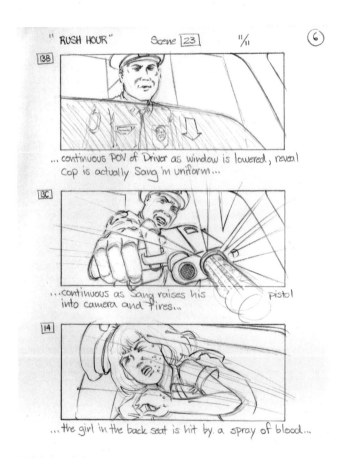

"RUSH HOUR"   Scene 23   11/11   ⑥

...continuous POV of Driver as window is lowered, reveal Cop is actually Sang in uniform...

...continuous as Sang raises his pistol into camera and fires...

...the girl in the back seat is hit by a spray of blood...

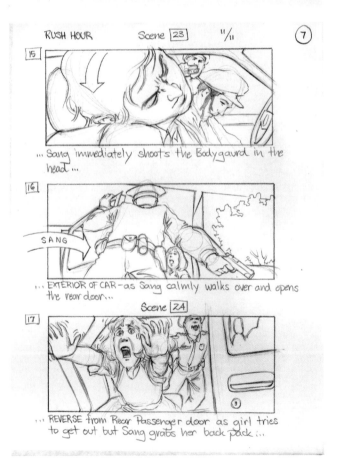

RUSH HOUR   Scene 23   11/11   ⑦

...Sang immediately shoots the Bodygaurd in the head...

SANG

...EXTERIOR OF CAR—as Sang calmly walks over and opens the rear door...

Scene 24

...REVERSE from Rear Passenger door as girl tries to get out but Sang grabs her back pack...

"RUSH HOUR"   Scene 24   11/11

...SANGS POV as Soon Young starts to kick him...

...Soon Youngs POV as she kicks Sang...

...a terriffied Soon Young runs across the front of the car...

"RUSH HOUR"   Scene 25   11/11

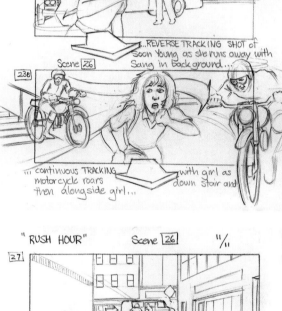

...CLOSE-UP of Sang as he turns toward the girl and smiles...

...REVERSE TRACKING SHOT of Soon Young as she runs away with Sang in background...

Scene 26

...continuous TRACKING motorcycle roars then alongside girl...

...with girl as down stair and

"RUSH HOUR"   Scene 26   11/11

...the motorcycle roars past and scoops up the girl...

...TRACKING SHOT with Motorcycle...

...REVERSE TRACKING SHOT of motorcycle...

"RUSH HOUR"   Scene 26   11/11

...a Van stops at the intersection and the motorcycle drives toward it...

...INTERIOR of Van as the girl is yanked in...

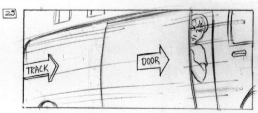

TRACK    DOOR

...TRACKING with Van as it speeds away, they slam the door shut.

**Lights, Camera, Action!**

I'm Detective Carter. Do you speaka any English? DO-YOU-UNDERSTAND-THE-WORDS-THAT-ARE-COMING-OUT-OF-MY-MOUTH?

CARTER: Don't you ever touch a black man's radio, boy! You can do that in China, but you can get your ass killed out here, man!

CARTER: Captain, I don't think this is funny. Now I'm serious, captain — I ain't playin'. You need to call the FBI and tell them you made a mistake.

CAPTAIN DIEL [on speakerphone]: I can't do that, Carter. I'm sure that you and Mr. Lee will have a nice time together.

CARTER: I'm warning you, man. You better call the FBI, or I'm gonna drop his ass off at Panda Express.

CAPTAIN DIEL: Drop this case, Carter, and you're suspended for two months without pay.

CARTER: All right, well, you can forget about being mayor then.

JOHNSON: Congratulations, Carter. Looks like you finally got yourself a partner.

*Lights, Camera, Action!*

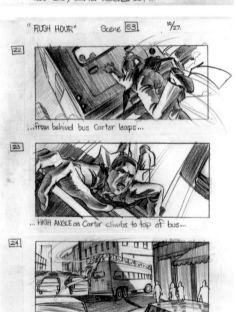

LEE: You must take me to see Consul Han right away.

CARTER: Man, just sit there and shut up! This ain't no democracy.

LEE: Yes, it is.

CARTER: No, it ain't. This is the United States of James Carter. I'm the president, I'm the emperor, I'm the king. I'm Michael Jackson, you Tito. Your ass belongs to me.

When I do a stunt like the one I had on the Hollywood sign, they really looked after me. The car, the speed, everything. Not like us. When I'm making a film [in Hong Kong] and we're rolling, we keep on shooting until well after sundown—there's always just one more shot. So we always get hurt. But on this movie the stunt coordinator really took care of me, and that made me more comfortable.

—JACKIE CHAN

**W**hat's good about this story is that it's about two under-dogs. Generally in this type of picture one guy is an established pro and the other guy is an outsider. Here you had two guys who were unwelcome in the rest of the story, and that gave us a lot of opportunities for character development and comedy.

**—PRODUCER JONATHAN GLICKMAN**

CARTER: Don't act like you don't
know what I'm talking about.
I'm gonna take all your asses
in right now if I don't get no
answers. . . . I see what's
going on here. Y'all trying
to play me like a fool. Y'all
think I'm a fool. All right,
look — Lee, go outside real
quick. It's gonna get a little
dangerous in here.

# THE CASE CENTERS ON THE IDENTITY of the mysterious Hong Kong

crime lord, Juntao, who—despite being dealt a devastating blow at the beginning of the film, when his vast cache of weapons and Chinese artifacts was confiscated by Lee—has long eluded the detective.

Juntao's whereabouts are unknown, but Carter and Lee are hot on the trail of his homicidal henchman, Sang, who carried out the kidnapping. The mystery deepens with the arrival of Han's old friend, Thomas Griffin, former commander of the Royal Hong Kong Police, who might not be what he seems. From star-studded Hollywood Boulevard to seedy Chinatown restaurants, Lee and Carter—the fastest hands in the East and the biggest mouth

in the West—leave no stone unturned as they hunt down the kidnappers. Their high-impact style of police work gets them branded as meddlers, and Carter is ordered off the case and Lee told to return to Hong Kong. But a young girl's life is at stake,

and the fledgling partners have ideas of their own. With the aid of the beautiful bomb expert Johnson, they initiate an explosive showdown at the Chinese Expo, where at last the deadly Juntao is revealed.

SANG: The drop will be made tonight. Eleven P.M. The amount will be fifty million dollars.

CARTER: Fifty million dollars? Man, who do you think you kidnapped? Chelsea Clinton?

SANG: In U.S. currency. Nothing bigger than a fifty.

CARTER: All right, all right, all right. Cool, cool, cool. Fifty million dollars, no problem, no problem.

SANG: I want twenty million in fifties.

CARTER: Twenty million in fifties.

SANG: Twenty million in twenties.

CARTER: Twenty million in twenties.

SANG: And ten million in tens.

CARTER: And ten million in tens. You want any fives with that?

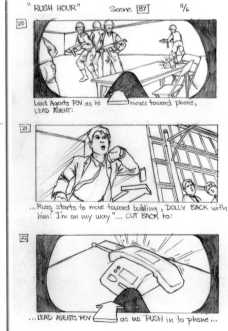

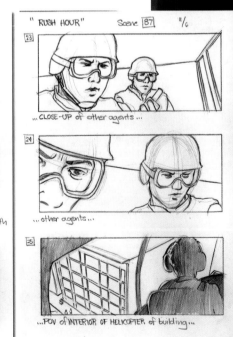

Chris Tucker is a master of verbal comedy. Jackie Chan is a master of physical comedy. Ultimately it was the perfect marriage. These two guys love each other. Chris makes Jackie laugh; Jackie makes Chris laugh. I don't think either understands a word the other is saying, but they're laughing and I just captured it on film.

**—BRETT RATNER**

I like the little stuff that makes people laugh. Like the scene when I'm trying to show Jackie how to sing "War" and he thinks he knows how, but he doesn't. So I teach him how to sing it, and we start dancing in the street in the middle of the night. That's my favorite scene.

**—CHRIS TUCKER**

Get the girl out
of here. Make
sure those two
don't leave.

I prefer a fighting scene to a dialogue scene. That's when I'm really scared. If there's a lot of dialogue the next day, I don't sleep the whole night. Because I not only have to remember my lines, I have to remember Chris's lines. And you know, Chris can do the same scene ten times with different dialogue!

—JACKIE CHAN

49

I got your bomb right here.

The fights are riotous slapstick set pieces: In the art museum finale, Chan fends off hordes of assassins while catching giant, priceless Ming vases as they tumble from their pedestals. As he demonstrates in picture after picture, he's willing to be stomped for art's sake.

—DAVID EDELSTEIN, *SLATE.COM*,
**SEPTEMBER 20, 1998**

CARTER: Hey, be cool, man. Hang on.

LEE: I can't hold on anymore!

CARTER: Hang on for about an hour. I'm gonna go
get the ambulance — I'll be right back.

LEE: What are you doing?

CARTER: Just hang on, man. I'll be right back...
Ah, I was just playin'.

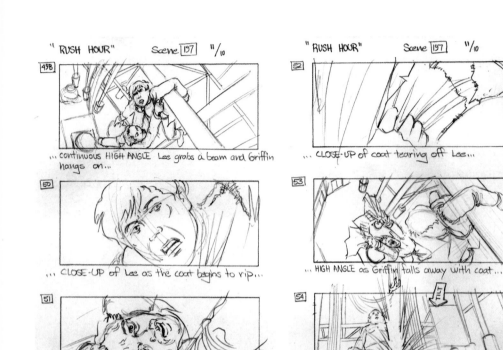

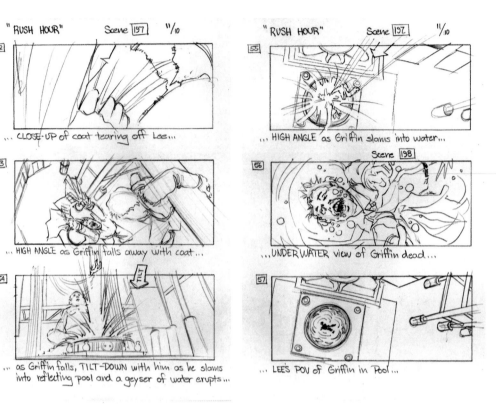

"RUSH HOUR"  Scene [197]  11/10

**49B** ...continuous HIGH ANGLE Lee grabs a beam and Griffin hangs on...

**50** ...CLOSE-UP of Lee as the coat begins to rip...

**51** ...CLOSE-UP of Griffin as he realizes coat is tearing...

"RUSH HOUR"  Scene [197]  11/10

**52** ...CLOSE-UP of coat tearing off Lee...

**53** ...HIGH ANGLE as Griffin falls away with coat...

**54** ...as Griffin falls, TILT-DOWN with him as he slams into reflecting pool and a geyser of water erupts...

"RUSH HOUR"  Scene [197]  11/10

**55** ...HIGH ANGLE as Griffin slams into water...

Scene [198]

**56** ...UNDERWATER view of Griffin dead...

**57** ...LEE'S POV of Griffin in Pool...

"RUSH HOUR"  Scene [199]  11/10

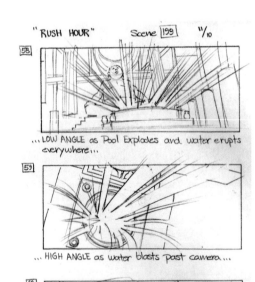

**58** ...LOW ANGLE as Pool Explodes and water erupts everywhere...

**59** ...HIGH ANGLE as water blasts past camera...

**60** ...people get drenched by a wave of water...

**61** ...CLOSE-UP of Lee, he starts to slip and calls out:"I'm falling!!"...

**62** ...CLOSE-UP on Carter as he sees Lee slipping...

**63A** ...Carter grabs the sash and pulls it past the Budda, TILT-UP to see...

**63B** ...continuous as we see Lee fall and hit sash...

**64** ...CLOSER of Lee sliding down sash...

**65** ...BOOM DOWN with Lee as he tries to slow down...

Before the first *Rush Hour*, I really had lost confidence in the American market. I didn't think an American audience would accept my kind of English, my kind of action. I figured I would just stay in Asia. But my manager pushed me, and I said, "Okay. This is my last try."

—JACKIE CHAN

CARTER: How long is this flight?

LEE: Fifteen hours.

CARTER: Fifteen hours? What are we
 gonna do for fifteen hours?

LEE [puts on headphones]: Huh! War!
 Uh! What is it good for. . .

CARTER: Oh, hell no! Stewardess!
 Get me another seat!

RUSH HOUR 2

HONG KONG / L.A. / LAS VEGAS

**CHIEF INSPECTOR LEE** of the Royal Hong Kong Police and LAPD detective James Carter arrive in Hong Kong for a vacation. Armed with his Chinese-English dictionary, Carter is looking forward to a much-needed vacation and to sampling some of the city's many exotic delights. But Lee, the ever-dedicated policeman, continues with his duties, frustrating Carter.

No sooner do they arrive than they are confronted with the biggest case of their careers—a bomb has exploded in the American Embassy, killing two U.S. Customs agents who had been investigating a money smuggling ring that is producing and shipping millions in "superbills," high-grade counterfeit U.S. $100 bills.

The Hong Kong police suspect the chief architect behind the blast is Ricky Tan, the elegant and cunning head of the Fu-Cang-Long Triad, the deadliest gang in China. Inspector Lee is assigned to crack the case, much to the chagrin of Carter, who is caught up in the events against his will and feels his vacation plans slipping away. For Lee the case is personal—Ricky Tan was once his father's partner on the Hong Kong police force and played a direct role in his father's death.

CARTER: Deng wa lu yun cai-shen wu.

LEE: You invited them to get naked and sacrifice a goat.

CARTER: I said that? Which word was for "goat"?

With the Hong Kong and U.S. authorities fighting over jurisdiction of the case, Lee and a reluctant Carter set off on their own to track down Tan. But this time it's Detective Carter who is the fish-out-of-water, and Lee now has the opportunity to teach him some lessons on his home turf. But in his own inimitable way, the fast-talking Carter has a few things to teach the locals as well!

LEE: These men are Triads. The most deadly
gang in China.

CARTER: You think they scare me? I'm from Los
Angeles. We invented gangs! Give me that badge.

LEE: No, you are a civilian. In Hong Kong,
*I* am Michael Jackson and *you* are Toto.

We cut out a karaoke scene from *Rush Hour* and knew we wanted to include a similar scene in the sequel. Karaoke is very serious business in Hong Kong. The notion of an American loudmouth like Chris's character singing in this revered environment was very funny.
—**PRODUCER ROGER BIRNBAUM**

# Carter: That's Tito. We had Toto for dinner last night.

CARTER: All right, listen up! All the Triads
and the ugly women on this side, and
all the fine women on this side, right now!

Carter walks to the edge of the roof...

REVERSE as Carter looks down to see...

CARTER'S POV of Lee hanging onto one of the scaffolding beams...

Carter turns to go help Lee when suddenly...

continuous Hu Li kicks Carter...

Carter flies off roof...

Carter lands on the same pole as Lee...

Hu Li looks down at Carter and Lee hanging from the pole...

CLOSE ON HU LI as she looks down...

HU LI'S POV of Carter and Lee...

Carter and Lee react to their situation...

Hu Li walks out of frame...

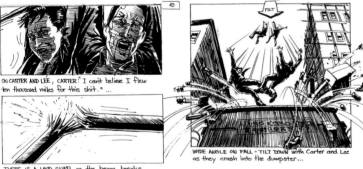

LOW ANGLE, Lee and Carter look down...

LEE AND CARTERS POV of Dumpster below them...

CLOSE ON BAMBOO BEAM as it begins to snap under their weight...

WIDE ANGLE on Carter and Lee as the beam bends even more...

CLOSE on Carter and Lee... CARTER: "All I wanted was a little mu-shu." LEE: ... you think that dumpster will break our fall?"...

CARTER AND LEES POV of Dumpster below...

ON CARTER AND LEE, CARTER: "I can't believe I flew ten thousand miles for this shit."...

THERE IS A LOUD SNAP as the beam breaks completely...

Carter and Lee fall

WIDE ANGLE ON FALL - TILT DOWN with Carter and Lee as they crash into the dumpster...

I work with him just like I would with any action coordinator. Jackie's been making movies longer than I've been alive, so I learn so much about the basics of stunt work and action from him. Typically you would have each fight sequence mapped out and designed and then you shoot a master and pick up the pieces. But here we design it on the day, piece by piece. I'm not going to tell Jackie how each kick and punch should be thrown. I just tell him where the scene starts and ends for the purpose of story telling. It's a much longer process, but the results are amazing.

—BRETT RATNER

Carter gets pushed onto the
same bamboo pole that Lee is
dangling from —

LEE: Don't worry, Chinese bamboo
     is very strong.

CARTER: Are you sure?

LEE: I'm sure. [as the lashing breaks
     and the two swing wildly downward]

For a lot of the stunts, you cannot physically do them without getting hurt. There's just no way to do it—the only way to not get hurt is not do them. The difference is to try not to get injured; there's a big difference between being hurt and being injured. Anytime guys are hitting each other, falling, and crashing—it hurts. You can't make an omelet without breaking a few eggs. How would you like to get beaten up by Jackie Chan? It hurts. But I can't think of anybody I'd rather have beating me up, because he knows how it feels.

**—EDDIE BRAUN**, stunt coordinator, *Rush Hour, Rush Hour 2, Rush Hour 3*

*ABOVE: Concept illustration by Terence Marsh.*

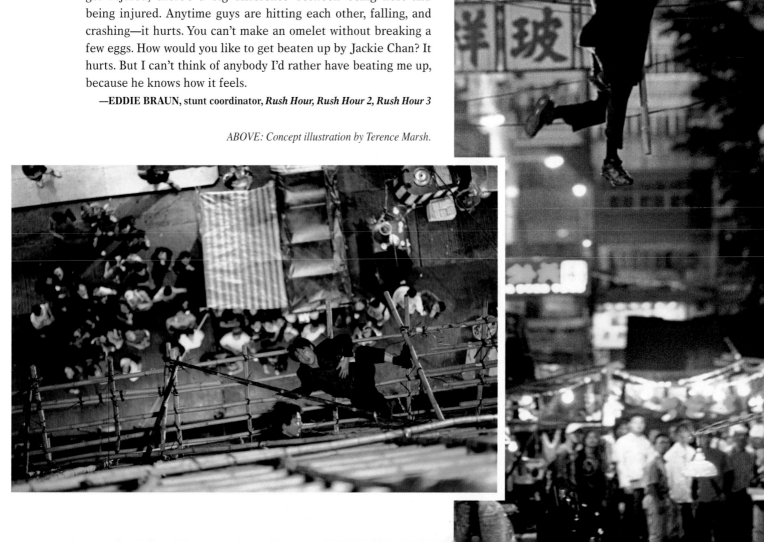

This place is off the hook!

LEE: What are you doing?

CARTER: She said I could have any
girl I want in here.

LEE: Well, hurry up!

CARTER: Man, what's wrong with you?
You don't jump in front of a black
man in a buffet line! Calm down!

LEE: That's Ricky Tan.

CARTER: That's Ricky Tan?
Man, that's a midget
in a bathrobe!

CARTER: I'm Lee's new muscle.
And don't let this robe
fool you. This is the
only color they had left.
Now I said get up!

I do creative comedy fighting, which is difficult. It's easy to do violence, to make blood come out and the audience gasp. My fight sequences are different. I want the audience to be dancing. It's a different kind of choreography.

—JACKIE CHAN

## AS LEE AND CARTER LEAD A FAST-PACED PURSUIT of Ricky Tan

and his gang, trying to locate the priceless plates used to print the counterfeit bills, they wreak havoc through a variety of Hong Kong locales, including a karaoke bar—where Carter teaches the gangster clientele how to sing the definitive version of the classic "Don't Stop 'Til You Get Enough"—the Heaven on Earth massage parlor, and a party on Tan's yacht cruising the waters of scenic Victoria Harbor.

Along the way they must contend with Tan's beautiful and deadly henchwoman Hu Li, billionaire hotel owner and key Ricky Tan associate Steven Reign, and the alluring, mysterious, and seemingly corrupt U.S. secret service agent Isabella Molina.

The action returns stateside for a brief detour through Los Angeles before climaxing in a spectacular, action-filled finale at the opening night of the Red Dragon Hotel and Casino on the Las Vegas Strip.

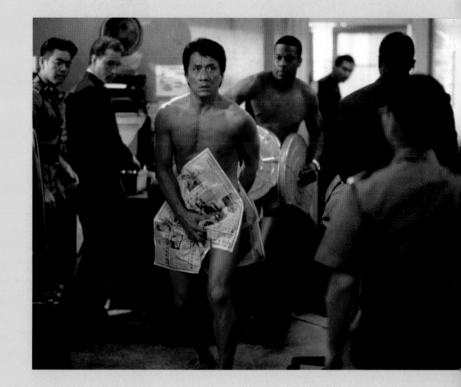

It was embarrassing. We were naked on the freeway, and I was almost hit by a truck. The truck driver pulled up and said, "Jackie Chan! Can I have your autograph?"

—JACKIE CHAN

## *Lights, Camera, Action!*

Jackie tricked me a lot of times in Hong Kong. One night we were at a restaurant that Jackie loves, and he had me try a special soup. I didn't know exactly what kind of soup it was, and finally the waiter came up to me and asked if I was enjoying the soup, which I said I was. He said, "Frog spit soup is our favorite dish." Jackie and I got in a little fight over it, but someone broke it up. I was eating some crazy stuff in Hong Kong, food that I don't want to admit that I ate!

—**CHRIS TUCKER**

*ABOVE: Concept illustration by Terence Marsh.*

I failed chemistry and logic and every math class I ever took in college, so it's very hard for me to explain why the *Rush Hour* films work as well as they do. As a kid I used to watch Gene Wilder and Richard Pryor comedies over and over, and when the movies would end and the lights came up, I just would sit there and imagine that Gene and Richard were still together somewhere having more fun. Their chemistry was so strong I simply couldn't imagine them apart. That's how I feel about Jackie Chan and Chris Tucker. A very talented and inspired director by the name of Brett Ratner had an idea to pair Tucker and Chan, and I've been working for him and writing for them ever since.

—**SCREENWRITER JEFF NATHANSON**

CARTER: Lee, let me introduce you to Carter's theory of criminal investigation: follow the rich white man.

LEE: Follow the rich white man?

CARTER: Exactly. Now you're learning. Every big crime has a rich white man behind it waiting for his cut.

"Lee? You Okay?"

Lee's eyes widen.

Isabella sets down coat, unbuttoning blouse.

Lee sweating -

"Slow down..."

Carter -

"What did you say?"

"Is it hot in here?"

CARTER POV - Lee turns away from window

When I heard about the Molina character, I told Brett Ratner that she and Lee must have a kissing scene or a love scene. Brett said, "You wish!"

**—JACKIE CHAN**

REVERSE - Carter and Lee reach the _____ bottom of the stairs and charge thru the door at _____ the bottom...

Carter and Lee round corner at bottom of stairs...

THEIR POV as they round _____ corner they come face to face with Zhao. Scene 74 EXT LOADING DOCK PLATFORM Steven Reign steps forward from his limo. STEVEN REIGN: "What is this?"

Ziyi Zhang is quite a chameleon. In contrast to her sweet looks, Hu Li becomes this brutal hard ass—it was a unique way for us to portray a villain.
—PRODUCER ARTHUR SARKISSIAN

Some apple?

EXT. LAS VEGAS BLVD - NIGHT, Lee's fingers come up thru grate at street level...

continuous, Lee pushes grate to side, then peers out at crowded Vegas street...

continuous, Carter comes out of hole as Lee helps him up...

LEE:"Vegas..." CARTER:"Lee... I just got and idea how someone could launder a hundred million dollars in cash." ...

LEE: Do you understand the words that are coming out of my mouth?

CARTER: Don't nobody understand the words that are comin' out of your mouth, man.

"RUSH HOUR II"        RED DRAGON HOTEL        Marc Vena

We needed to up the stakes in this one. And that wasn't going to be easy considering that in *Rush Hour* a little girl's life was on the line. So we raised the emotional ante by creating a character that would explain Lee's motivation and also explain why Carter is who he is—both had fathers who were cops and were killed in the line of duty. Once Carter realizes that Lee wants this case in order to basically protect his father's legacy and get to the bottom of what he went down for, he jumps on board to help his friend. It brings heart to the story.

**—BRETT RATNER**

I wanted a very Vegas-y type of guy for the role of Steven Reign, and Alan King is the perfect guy to own a casino. I modeled him partly after a Steve Wynn and Donald Trump type of character. You see the showman and entrepreneur side of him very clearly. But you also see that inside, this guy is as tough as nails.

—BRETT RATNER

*ABOVE and BELOW: Concept illustrations by Terence Marsh.*

**V**egas is my town. Now that I have the key to the city, they have to let me in any place I go. I wish Sammy Davis, Jr., were here to see this!
—**CHRIS TUCKER**

CARTER: Lee! What are you doing?

LEE: Dancing.

CARTER: Dancing! Man, I'm up
    here working, putting my
    life on the line, and you
    up here messing around,
    dancing with some bimbo...
    Does she have a friend?

## Lights, Camera, Action!

Long after saner, less brilliant physical actors would have retired, Chan still has some extraordinary moves, sliding and ducking as if there's no such thing as gravity.

—ROBERT KOEHLER,
*VARIETY*, JULY 30, 2001

Having Jackie on the film is like having that veteran player on a sports team. They show up on time, they know what they're doing and they always put their all into it. Plus he's an amazing physical comedian, the same way Keaton and Chaplin were. He does things you don't think a human being can do.

—**PRODUCER JAY STERN**

```
HU LI: Inspector Lee, this is
    a ying-tao grenade. Please
    follow me, or I'll push this
    detonator and blow thirty-two
    teeth into your brain.
```

I ain't gonna crap out!

*RIGHT: Restaurateur Michael Chow (Mr. Chow), with dark glasses, has appeared in all three* Rush Hour *movies.*

Don't move. U.S. Secret Service — you're under arrest!

CARTER: I'm not gonna hold back on you this time because you're a woman. I'm gonna pretend you a man. A very beautiful man with a perfect body who I'd like to take to the movies.

CARTER: We could have been a good couple. We could have had something special. But you one crazy-ass bitch!

①

INT PENTHOUSE SUITE - NIGHT
Lee and Carter kick Ricky Tam out window...

②

continuous, as he falls...

REVERSE as Ricky Tam crashes thru window...

Ricky Tam falls away from camera toward street...

5A

continuous, as Ricky Tams body slams into the top of a cab...

EXT OF HOTEL as Tam flies out window, TILT-DOWN with him...

Lee and Carter walk up to window and look down...

③

Lee and Carters POV thru broken window...

④

REVERSE - Behind Hu Li we see she's holding a bomb...

⑤

CLOSE ON HU LI as she holds up bomb...

as Lee and Carter look down, Hu Li walks into the room behind them...CARTER: "I don't know about you, but I need a wine cooler."... THEY TURN when they hear Hu Li walk in...

CARTER AND LEE'S POV of HU LI: (in Chinese) "We'll go together, Inspector."

CARTER: "Bomb!!" LEE: "Follow me..."

Carter and Lee turn around to see Hu Li...

Lee understands what she just said. CARTER: "Please tell me she just asked for a ride to the airport."...

Lee spins around and runs toward window as he removes his coat, Carter hesitates and then follows...

⑥

continuous, as they run ———— toward window...

Carter and Lee loop their coats over the wire...

continuous, they slide down cable...

⑦

CUT TO... PUSH IN on HuLi as we here an audible "CLICK"... then silence...

WIDE ANGLE as Lee and Carter slide toward camera, there's an EXPLOSION...

WIDE ANGLE, LOOKING DOWN STRIP – Carter and Lee slide down thru debris...

⑧

REVERSE TRACK with they slide down...   TRACK   Lee and Carter as

REVERSE     as Carter and Lee slide past they smash into lights...

Lee and Carter smash thru the lanterns...

⑨

THE CROWD BELOW reacts to what Carter and Lee are doing...

THE CABLE SNAPS!...

LEE and CARTER fly thru frame...

⑩

WIDE ANGLE ON SCENE as Carter and Lee swing out and under banner post...

LONG LENS against building as Lee and Carter swing toward camera - debris and lanterns fall in the background...

CLOSE ON     LINES as they wrap around cross beam...

HIGH ANGLE [BLUE SCREEN] of Carter and Lee as they are flipped over pole...

WIDE ANGLE ON SCENE as they are flipped over beam...

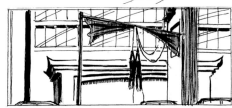

WIDE ANGLE on Strip as pole PIVOTS over street...

That wasn't so bad!

**RH2: Hong Kong / L.A. / Las Vegas**

CARTER: Will you stop acting like a cop
for one second, man, and live it
up? There's gotta be something you
want. Come on, think about it!

LEE: I always wanted to go to Madison
Square Garden, see the Knicks play.

CARTER: New York City?

LEE: First class.

CARTER: The Plaza Hotel.

LEE: Maybe some moo shu.

CARTER: Amen to that, brother.

LEE: So what do you say?

CARTER: You know what, man? I could
use another vacation.

RUSH HOUR 3

L.A. / PARIS

**MISFIT PARTNERS** from East and West, Lee and Carter, take on the Chinese Triad, an ancient global crime empire, as they attempt to unravel the mystery of *Shy Shen*, or "Spirit of Death"—the Triad's most closely guarded secret. No one knows exactly what the elusive *Shy Shen* is, but word that it's about to go public at the meeting of the World Criminal Court has a network of underworld assassins on a killing spree.

Lee and Carter haven't been on speaking terms for years, not since Carter "accidentally" shot Lee's girlfriend and dashed his romantic dreams. But their paths cross again when Lee arrives in Los Angeles, charged with protecting his friend and ally Ambassador Han, who is about to expose the *Shy Shen* at the World Criminal Court, shattering an empire of extortion, drug, sex, and slavery rings around the world.

Their reunion gets off to a rocky start though. While trying to assist Lee foil an assassination attempt on Han's life, Carter inadvertently helps the Triad gunman escape. Now Han, fighting for his life in a hospital bed, as well as his daughter, Soo Yung, are *Shy Shen* targets…and chances are they won't survive for long. Reluctantly, the duo team up once again to bring the Triad down. They don't have much information to go on until a second attempt on Han's life is made by French-speaking Asian assassins, and the French Foreign Minister narrowly escapes death in a car explosion.

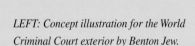

*LEFT: Concept illustration for the World Criminal Court exterior by Benton Jew.*

*Lights, Camera, Action!*

CARTER: Lee, it's me, and we are on for tonight! I just picked up two Russian girls.

LEE: Carter, I can't talk now. I'm in the car with Ambassador Han.

CARTER: Tell Han he can watch!

*BELOW: Concept illustration by Daren Dochterman.*

AMBASSADOR HAN:

The Triad society is built on secrecy. Nobody knows who these men are—who controls them—who leads them. Nobody has known for five hundred years. But today I stand before you with a secret of my own... After years of searching, I believe I have finally located *Shy Shen.*

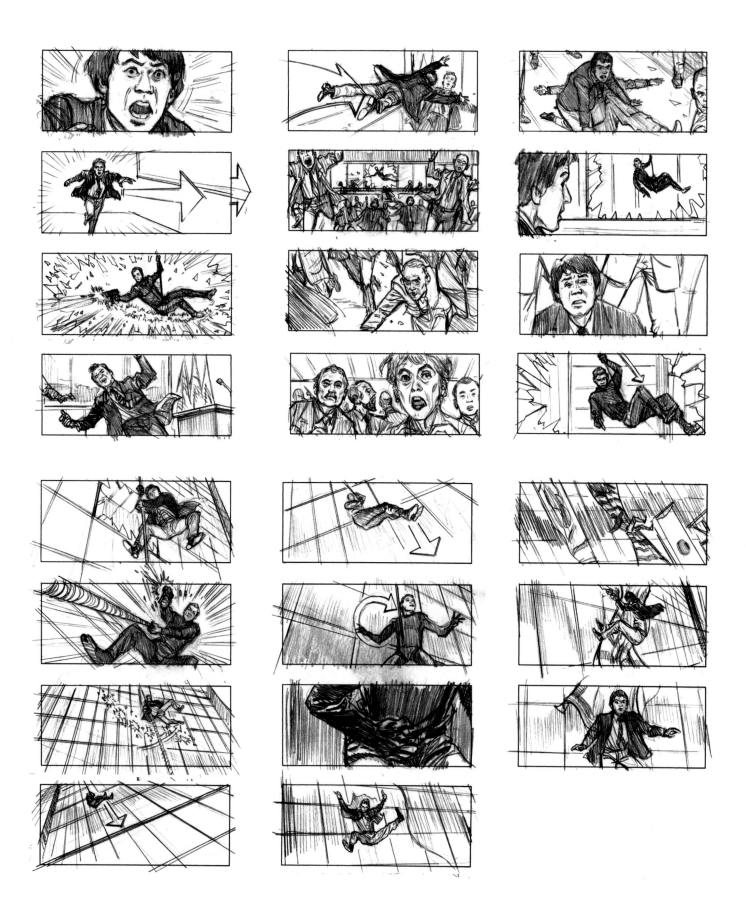

When we were watching the first set of dailies, we thought, Wow, this looks a lot closer to a movie like *Three Days of the Condor* than it does to *Rush Hour 2*. And that was great. We wanted it to feel a lot more gritty. It makes the thriller aspect more thrilling, and it makes the comedy even funnier because it's up against something that is so real.

—**PRODUCER JONATHAN GLICKMAN**

CARTER: That's right, Lee, for the last three years I've studied the ancient teachings of Buddha every night, earned two black belts in the wushu martial arts, and spent every afternoon at the Hong Kong Gardens Massage Parlor at Pico and Bundy. I am half Chinese.

un Ming Ming. Great guy. Nicest guy you'll ever meet, but the tallest guy I've ever seen in my life. Taller than any basketball player I've ever seen. We have this big fight in the film. I go into this karate school and disrespect the tradition of the school—and out comes this big giant and basically whups me and Jackie's ass.

—CHRIS TUCKER

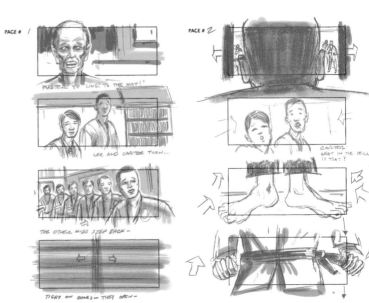

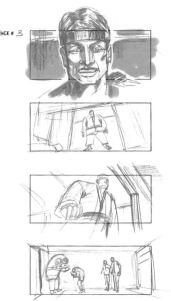

PAGE # 3

PAGE # 4

MASTER YU: LEAVE NOW OR PREPARE TO FIGHT!

CARTER: I THINK THIS BOY IS ON STEROIDS. HE'S GOT A HEAD LIKE BARRY BONDS.

MASTER YU: "ONE."

PAGE # 5

CARTER: MAYBE LING SHOULD PEE IN A CUP.

MASTER YU: TWO!

CARTER: YOU THINK I'M SCARED OF A GIANT ASIAN! PROBABLY SLOWER THAN GODZILLA! COME ON, LING. BRING IT ON.

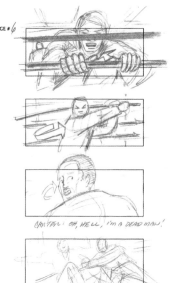

PAGE # 6

CARTER: OH, HELL, I'M A DEAD MAN.

SOO YUNG: I want you both to promise me something. I want you to find the man who did this to him. I want you to find him, because I don't think he'll stop until my father is dead.

Brett truly loves the action-comedy genre. He grew up with *Beverly Hills Cop* and *48 Hours* as the sort of movies that made him want to be a filmmaker. He loves being around these kinds of sets. He loves the size of these films. And so he is exactly the guy to tackle something this large with this much action and this much comedy.

—SCREENWRITER JEFF NATHANSON

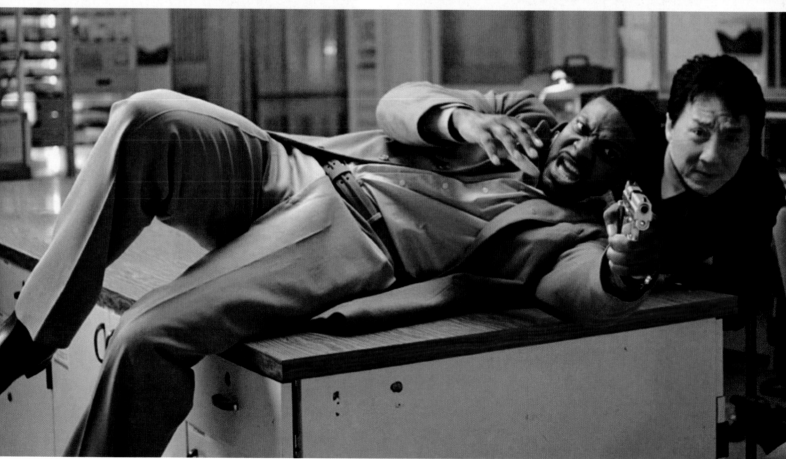

Sister, you tell this piece of "S-word" that I will personally "F-word" him up!

REYNARD: I'm getting you out of Los
        Angeles. It's not safe for you —
        for any of the members of the World
        Court. My plane is waiting.

The first idea for *Rush Hour 3* was to film in Hawaii, which was good for me. But Chris didn't like it. He thought we should film outside the U.S. He suggested Bangkok, which I didn't like. Then Brett said, "Let's go to Paris." And we all agreed. Beautiful clothing, beautiful country, beautiful women, beautiful cars. Clean, beautiful action—that's *Rush Hour 3*.

—JACKIE CHAN

CARTER: We have an assassin in custody who only speaks French, a limo blows up at the French Consulate, and the next meeting of the World Court is in Paris two days from now.

LEE: Carter, are you thinking what I'm thinking?

CARTER: We go to Fiji. We hide out for a year, maybe change our names — get jobs as bartenders. I'll call you Kiko.

**IT'S CLEAR** the *Shy Shen* trail leads to Paris, so Lee and Carter have no choice but to head for the City of Lights, where they find themselves strangers in a strange land, full of churlish cabbies, sadistic police captains, and stunning showgirls.

The Triad will stop at nothing to protect the secret of *Shy Shen*, and on French soil things really start to heat up—especially when it turns out that the fearless assassin who runs the Triad is none other than Lee's wayward brother, Kenji. Will Lee's blood ties be stronger than his sense of duty? Will he and Carter be able to save Han and Soo Yung? Will Carter be able to keep his hands off the French girls long enough to help?

Excuse me, gentlemen, my name is Captain Revi of
the F.S.P. Would you please step this way?

**B**rett was always telling me that he would like to have me appear in one of his movies. One day he said he was thinking of making *Rush Hour 3* with a sequence in Paris, and he would like very much to write a little part for me. When he came to Paris, he said, "Yes, I really want you to do it," and that's how I happened to be in the film.

—ROMAN POLANSKI (CAPTAIN REVI)

**R**oman Polanski invited me to his home, and he had pulled everything out of his closet in case there was something I might think would be right for his character. We talked a lot about it, even down to the details of the tie. Earlier I had found in a French costume house this really ratty jacket that I thought, well, even though I don't know if the measurements are correct, I'll bring it just in case. He fell in love with that jacket. He was like, "This is so perfect." So he begins to run his lines with me in the outfit, and he gets his body language inspired by the costume, and he starts to become the character right before my very eyes.

—COSTUME DESIGNER BETSY HEIMANN

RF

POLICE

**COMMISSAIRE DE POLICE**

Les Autorités Civiles et Militaires sont invitées à LAISSER PASSER ET CIRCULER LIBREMENT le titulaire de la présente carte qui est autorisé à requérir l'assistance de la force publique pour les besoins du service.

**MINISTERE DE L'INTERIEUR**
DIRECTION GENERALE DE LA POLICE NATIONALE

LEE: Stay focused, Carter. We're looking for Genevieve.

CARTER: Split up. I'll take the women.

**R**ush Hour 3 needs a big city. It needs a grand scale. Paris is a character unto its own. The people, the skyline, the fountains, the architecture, the personality, the charm, the danger, the chic-ness of it all are so important to the story. They're part of the plot.

**—BRETT RATNER**

*BELOW: Illustration by Benton Jew.*

Casting Noémie was very difficult. We were concerned that we weren't going to find somebody sexy who could pull off the part of an English-speaking French person who has an enormous amount of dialogue and has to go head-to-head with Chris. It was a very extensive casting process, but when we saw her screen test, we knew we'd found her. She's so sexy onscreen. And Chris was so comfortable with her from minute one. She really gives him a run for his money.

**—PRODUCER JONATHAN GLICKMAN**

GENEVIEVE: Mr. Carter...
    it appears you have
    brought me luck.

CARTER: I'd rather bring
    you breakfast in bed.

**Lights, Camera, Action!**

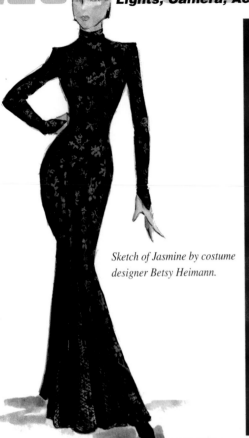

*Sketch of Jasmine by costume designer Betsy Heimann.*

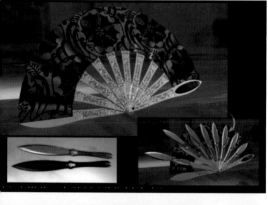

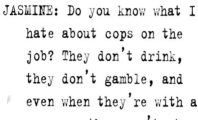

JASMINE: Do you know what I hate about cops on the job? They don't drink, they don't gamble, and even when they're with a woman — they can't stop thinking about getting their man... Come upstairs, cop. I'll give you what you want.

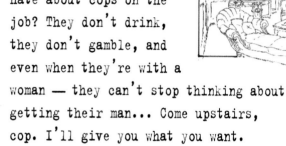

*LEFT: Fan illustrations by Chris Ross. ABOVE: Sketch of Jasmine's boudoir by Ed Verreaux.*

Someone is going to die here tonight.

Never in my life did I imagine that I would fight the famous Jackie Chan. I had never done an action movie. I couldn't imagine I was going to beat him up. It's hard to be an action star, but I enjoyed it very much. I got bruises all over my body. The makeup artist was so sweet, putting cream all over me, but when I saw myself in the mirror that night, I was amazed at how many bruises I had. I hadn't even noticed.
—**YOUKI KUDOH (JASMINE)**

That's my boy! Go for it, Lee! Come on, crouching tiger, don't hide that dragon!

GEORGE: Please, I can't do this!
I'm scared!

CARTER: You watch American
movies... Who do you like
— name an action hero!

GEORGE: I don't know! Matt Damon!

CARTER: Okay. You're Matt Damon!
You're a super-spy!

GEORGE: I'm Matt Damon! I'm a
super-spy!

Jackie's the most humble man I've met. I only realized how huge he was when we were in Paris. I knew he was popular—he's a great actor—but it was crazy on the streets of Paris. Everybody recognized him. I thought I had the Beatles in my cab.

—YVAN ATTAL (GEORGE)

**Lights, Camera, Action!**

*Storyboards by Piere-Emmanuel Chatiliez.*

Making the third *Rush Hour* film is the hardest thing I've ever done, because with *Rush Hour 2*, we had to try to top *Rush Hour*. Now we have to try to do something that we didn't do in the first two movies. Chris, Jackie, and I are constantly challenging each other. How do we do this differently? How do we do something that's going to take us to the next level?

—BRETT RATNER

OVER JACKIES SHOULDER
ASHE HANGS ON TO CHRIS.

ON REAR OF CAR AND MOTORCYCLE
AS ...

...MOTOTRCYCLE COMES IN FAST...

...ON THEIR REACTIONS.

REVERSE : LONGER LENS AS
MOTORCYCLE BEARS DOWN
ON CHRIS...

137

I told you we should have gone to Fiji!

CARTER: Lee, you know this clown?

KENJI: Go on, Lee, tell him who I am. Don't be shy — introduce him to your *Shyong Dih*.

CARTER: *Shyong Dih*? Your brother?

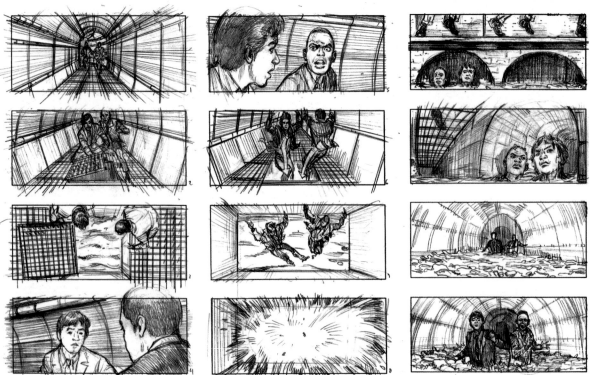

The good thing about the *Rush Hour* franchise is everybody has worked with each other from day one, since 1997. So you don't have to bring anyone up to speed—they're just part of the family.

**—PRODUCER ARTHUR SARKISSIAN**

When you go from the top of the Eiffel Tower to the sewers of Paris, you really have hit the highs and lows of it all. We took advantage of the best the city has to offer, the mystique of Paris.

**—SECOND UNIT DIRECTOR
CONRAD PALMISANO**

CARTER: We need a big suite. Two beds. Two showers. A massage therapist, some new clothes, and a case of Old Spice.

Bitch.

CARTER: How come you never told me about Kenji?

LEE: It was none of your business.

CARTER: In case you missed it, people are trying to kill me! They hit me, shoot at me, call me names — so don't tell me this is none of my business!

Chris Tucker is a very funny man. He's very fast; he has a great sense of timing and a good sense of humor and a good sense for absurdity, which works very well in this film. And Jackie Chan is a genius when it comes to action. He also has a very warm personality, which comes off wonderfully onscreen. Together the two are brilliant. It's a wonderfully humorous and absurd combination of intelligence and energies, and I think it's just a brilliant idea to get them together.

—MAX VON SYDOW (REYNARD)

REYNARD: *Shy Shen* isn't a person. It's a list.

LEE: A list?

REYNARD: Yes... Thirteen names are inscribed on a list known as *Shy Shen* — a list that has been passed down and kept secret from generation to generation.

LEE: If the names on that list were ever to get out...

REYNARD: Their secret society wouldn't be so secret anymore. They'd all end up in jail — or dead.

LEE: And the list is somewhere in Paris?

REYNARD: A woman named Genevieve made contact with Ambassador Han. We believe she knows where it is... Get to the girl before the Triads do — and you get *Shy Shen*.

CARTER: All of you — out of those clothes right now! Come on, ladies, we have work to do!

*FAR LEFT: Concept illustration of the Folies dressing room by Benton Jew.*

**Lights, Camera, Action!**

Genevieve runs with the Triads. They've got all the money in the world, so she had to look chic and sophisticated and gorgeous.

I wanted to use as many French things as I could. I had an assistant in Paris go to all the locations mentioned in the script with her camera and take pictures of who was going to this club, who was in the lobby of the Plaza, what does the concierge wear, what does the housekeeper wear. We amassed all of our research that way, through actual photographs of the real people.

—COSTUME DESIGNER BETSY HEIMANN

*Costume illustrations
by Betsy Heimann.*

**Lights, Camera, Action!**

This was the hardest casting that I've done on any movie, because Brett really wanted the girls to look like the shows that he saw in Paris. And in the shows in Paris, they all match identically. I knew I needed tall girls, leggy girls, but to find girls that matched body-wise was not so easy. I think I saw 450 girls to get only ten.

**—CHOREOGRAPHER MARGUERITE DERRICKS**

*ABOVE: Concept illustration by Daren Dochterman.*

**W**orking with Brett on this number, for me, was like a dream. I've talked to a lot of the older divas like Cyd Charisse and Ann Miller, and they talked about what it was like to create dance for film back in the day when they really took the time to do it right. One time while we were shooting, Brett stopped everything on the set for four and a half hours to make sure that this piece was lit beautifully and properly. You don't often get that. When I looked at the film, I just wanted to just cry, because it was so beautiful. He shot it like Gene Kelly and Bob Fosse shot their movies. Brett took the time to make sure the dance was really captured. It's beautiful, and he gets it. It was an honor to work with a director who shot my choreography with such care.

—CHOREOGRAPHER MARGUERITE DERRICKS

*RIGHT: Prop program for Genevieve's show by graphic artist Susan A. Burig.*

**THE ASSASSIN KENJI** and his striking, knife-throwing accomplice, Jasmine, dog the fast-talking, fast-kicking detectives' every step as they race to unravel the intentions of the powerful Varden Reynard, head of the World Criminal Court, and the beautiful showgirl Genevieve, who might hold the key to the entire mystery.

Carter and Lee rumble their way though Paris in a tour that includes the exclusive underground Club La Passe, the ancient Parisian sewers, the legendary, show-stopping Théâtre des Champs-Élysées, and a final death-defying face-off high atop the Eiffel Tower, where Carter and Lee battle to settle personal scores and risk everything to crush a global crime syndicate.

GENEVIEVE: You don't get it. I'm one of them. And if I'm dead — you're dead.

*ABOVE: Concept illustrations for Jasmine's knives by Chris Ross.*

CARTER: You are a sick man, Lee. I was just rounding second base — tell him, Genevieve!

LEE: I was trying to save your life!

CARTER: You couldn't wait three minutes! Now the date is over! I hope you're happy!

GEORGE: Yesterday was
    amazing. The guns,
    the shooting — now
    I understand what it
    is to be American.

*BELOW: Daren Dochterman's concept
illustration of George's apartment.*

I am Shy Shen.

Noémie has a street quality to her. She brings a toughness and a kind of surly vulnerability to the role of Genevieve. For the movie, we shaved her head, and I was blown away at how beautiful she was without any hair. In fact, I think she's more stunning without hair than she is with.

**—PRODUCER ANDREW Z. DAVIS**

Max von Sydow is a great guy. When he comes on the set it's like King Arthur is coming on the set. I was almost scared to talk to him. I was calling him Mister von Sydow. And he said, "No, call me Max." And once he said that, I was like, "Max, what's up?!"

—CHRIS TUCKER

*ABOVE: Daren Dochterman's concept illustration of Reynard's office.*

REYNARD: Look at that. Thirteen
    names linked to centuries
    of tradition. The only real
    proof that their secret world
    exists.

REYNARD (in Chinese): *Kill them.*

It starts with a conversation between Jackie, Brett, Connie Palmisano, who's the second unit director and U.S. stunt coordinator, myself, and Jeff Nathanson, the writer. We throw out a bunch of ideas and Jackie looks at what Jeff has written and says, "Let me talk to my guys and see what I can come up with." So they hide themselves in a dark room somewhere—we don't know where that is, it's a secret lair that only Chinese people are admitted to—and they call us a few days later and say, "Okay, come and see this." And they go through the scene. Usually one of the Chinese guys plays Chris and one of the guys plays Jackie. It's kind of like live editing. Brett will say, "You know, I like this, but Jackie, what if you went over the guy's head?" And Jackie will say, "Well, maybe not over the head; maybe I'll jump instead." Then we'll go away, and they'll come back and show us another version. And they videotape it and talk about it.

On the day we're shooting, the scene still changes, because the other actors and the camera people are there. It's constantly evolving, constantly getting better. And that's the great thing. It's like improvisation. It really feels like you're bringing together great jazz musicians who all play different instruments, and when they come together it creates a unique thing that none of us can create by ourselves.

**—PRODUCER ANDREW Z. DAVIS**

believe we did things on the Eiffel
Tower that have never been done
before.

**—SECOND UNIT DIRECTOR
CONRAD PALMISANO**

I n China you wear white to a funeral. White is the color of death. So we wanted Kenji to wear white, because he is the bearer of death for Jackie Chan. And in the end, when all the Triads descend on the Eiffel Tower, they're all wearing white, because this is a funeral— Jackie's funeral—for them.

—COSTUME DESIGNER
BETSY HEIMANN

There is a Philips light bulb color that is only available to the Eiffel Tower. If you're going to truly represent the Eiffel Tower, you need to use this color. So for our Eiffel Tower sets, we wanted to match the girders and the color of the light, so we made sure to use these very special bulbs.

**—CINEMATOGRAPHER J. MICHAEL MURO**

*ABOVE and BELOW: Rough sketches by Ed Verreaux. RIGHT: (left to right) Second Unit Director Conrad Palmisano and Stunt Coordinator Eddie Braun talk with Jackie Chan. BELOW RIGHT: Blueprint by Paul Sonski.*

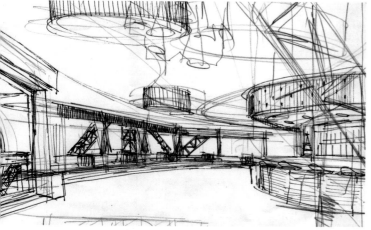

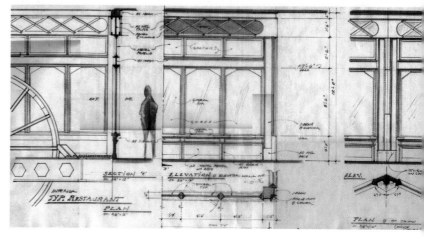

**Lights, Camera, Action!**

WWW.PE-CHATILIEZ.COM

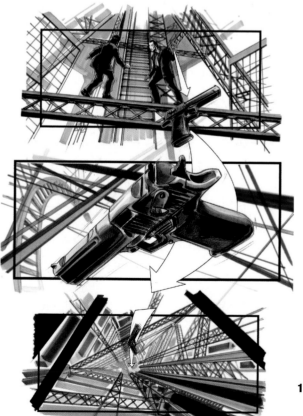

175

KENJI: Tonight I lose a brother.

**Lights, Camera, Action!**

CARTER: Stay cool, lady. This
doesn't have to end this way.

JASMINE: And how would you like
it to end?

CARTER: Any chance of you
committing suicide?

Carter's POV of Soo Yung...

ALTERNATE Soo Yung hanging....

.Carter climbs out window.

.Camera booms up over elevator shaft..

Wide Shot, Carter moves out....

Carter looks down....

CARTER: Lee... reel me in!
    Lee, hurry. BLACK PEOPLE
    DON'T FLY!

LEE: Carter... hold on!

CARTER: ARE YOU CRAZY?!

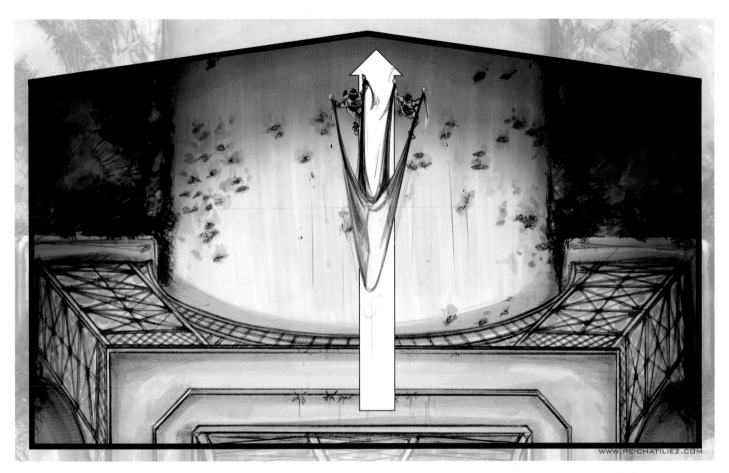

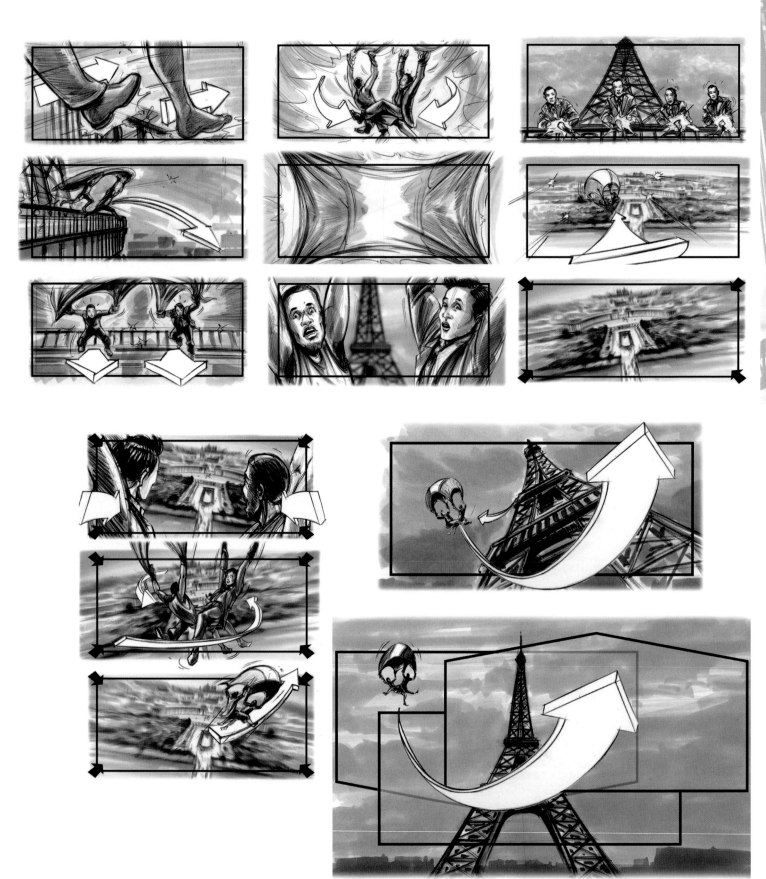

REYNARD: Get your hands up...
You can't fight tradition.

Case closed.

Lee... you go this way —

And I go that way —

# RUSH HOUR
*Lights, Camera, Action!*

## Acknowledgments

We wish to thank the following for their special contributions to this book:

*From the* Rush Hour *Production Team:* Brett Ratner, Jackie Chan, Chris Tucker, Jeff Nathanson, Guy Adan, Glen Wilson, Ed Verreaux, Chad Frey, Brad Einhorn, Kate Sullivan, Matt McKee, Betsy Heimann, and Adam Howard. A note of special gratitude to Associate Producer David Gorder for his enthusiastic initiative and his invaluable help in coordinating all aspects of this book.

*Artists who shared their talent:* Susan Burig, Pierre-Emmanuel Chatiliez, Daren Dochterman, Warren Drummond, Benton Jew, Jim Magdaleno, Terence Marsh, David Negron Jr., Chris Ross, and Paul Sonski.

*At New Line Cinema:* David Imhoff, John Mayo, Emily Glatter, Ryan Miningham, Travis Topa, Amy Rivera, Stacy Osugi, and Russell Schwartz.

And special thanks to Timothy Shaner at Night and Day Design (nightanddaydesign.biz) for his exciting design and editorial contributions, and to the Newmarket team, including Frank DeMaio, Paul Sugarman, Heidi Sachner, Harry Burton, Linda Carbone, Edward McPherson, and Tracey Bussell.

—Esther Margolis, Publisher, and
Keith Hollaman, Executive Editor,
Newmarket Press